LIVING WITH
LESS STUFF

LIVING WITH LESS STUFF

MARIA WARD, M.A.

Names: Ward, Maria, author

Title: Living with Less Stuff / Maria Ward

Cover design by Teressa J. Martin

I dedicate this book to my husband, Terry, who has given me lots of practice decluttering and organizing. Thank you for all your encouragement during our fifty plus years of marriage.

Contents

Introduction

Whether you identify yourself as a retiree, senior citizen, baby boomer or older adult, this book is for you.

When we are young, we spend our lives accumulating stuff - house, cars, boats, furniture, recreational items, gadgets, electronics, art, jewelry and more. Now that we don't work anymore, and spend more time at home, the stuff starts irritating us. It gets in the way, needs to be cleaned or fixed, and gives us little pleasure. It is now time to find new homes for our excess stuff. Finding new homes could mean giving memorabilia to relatives and friends, selling stuff to interested parties, contributing to charities, or just tossing useless things into the trash.

The following chapters were published in the monthly Senior Living Section of the Houston Chronicle from 2016 to 2019. There are a few minor changes from the Houston Chronicle publications in this book.

Most of the techniques mentioned in the book are creations from my own life. I have always been an organizer. As a child, I would organize and reorganize drawers and boxes trying to maximize the space I had. In school, I always was the neatest student, focusing on my current subject, but planning how I would complete projects and papers timely and efficiently. After I got married, my husband would kid me and say if he could not find me, he knew I was in one of our closets, organizing. I received my BBA degree from Wichita State University in Human Resources. When I started working in business, my employers often commented on how organized and efficient I was. I would set up systems for routine processing that would be adapted by the company.

While taking time off from work to complete my MA degree through Our Lady of the Lake University, I set up an organizing business and joined the local professional organizers group. I returned to Human Resources after completing my Master's degree.

Now that I have retired, I have started writing down some of my techniques and mythology and offering organizing classes through Lone Star College – Academy for Livelong Learning. In 2016, I started writing a monthly column for the Senior Living Section of the Houston Chronicle entitled, "Staying Organized."

In this book, I am taking the collection of articles from the monthly column and presenting them for you to ponder and apply to your life to make it easier.

Hope you enjoy it and find the organizing and uncluttering sections applicable to your retirement life needs.

Maria Ward

I.
Manage Wardrobe Easily with Closet Organization

Whether you have a big selection of clothes or a small one, maintaining an organized closet allows you to manage your wardrobe easily.

Seniors often save their old clothes too long. It is much better to buy some new crisp pieces rather than wear aged clothes from way back when, because they are still good to you!

To stay organized in your closet, sort all your clothes by type: pants, skirts, shirts, pajamas, jackets, dresses, sweaters, etc. Hang up everything except for underwear. Turn all the clothes in the same direction. Also, sort all your shoes by type, turning them all in the same direction.

If you are looking for a little more organization, use different types of hangers for your clothes. As an example: for pants, use wire hanger with a paper tube, for blouses use light wire hangers, for sweaters and jackets, use store-bought plastic hangers, for skirts, use plastic hangers with clips, for tee shirts, use a dry cleaner hanger, etc. The idea is to have a distinct hanger for different clothes items.

If you want to go to extremes, place items you plan to wear again in the front of the grouping and clean items in the back of the grouping. You will soon notice the clothes in the middle of the grouping may seldom get worn. It may be time to consider giving those clothing items you do not wear to a charity.

It is soothing to look at your closet, and everything is in order. Make sure you follow the plan every day.

2.
Meal Planning Does Not Have to be Difficult

Thinking about all the meals a person prepares is mind boggling. Not only do you have to decide what you want to have for meals, but you have to either go to the grocery store to buy the ingredients or stop at a fast food joint to pick up the food. When you go out to eat, you still need to decide what is the best choice for your mood.

Many seniors don't like to cook for just one or two, so they will eat out or grab whatever comes to mind. Often the spur of the moment meal is not so healthy.

So, what is the solution? Easy! At the end of each meal, start thinking about and gathering the food for the next meal. I have often heard people say: You just finished eating and you are already thinking about the next meal? Actually, that is a very good idea! Once you finish lunch, start thinking what you will need for dinner. Start thinking about what you have on hand. If for some reason, there are missing items, you still have time to go to the store. Or if you are eating out, you can look up the menu online and pick something healthy in advance.

Even though this may seem excessive, thinking about food so much, it is just good planning. It is great to know what you will have for dinner before your stomach says it is time to eat.

As a dedicated organizer, you will take one day a week to make trays that can be frozen and warmed up in the oven or microwave. You can have meals ready to eat with no preparation. When holidays arrive, you may end up with plenty of leftovers for trays. If you prefer to purchase freshly prepared meals, grocery stores and food outlets sell healthy individual meal choices.

By planning ahead, you will have healthy, fulfilling meals that will reduce the stress related to figuring out what to eat. Maybe even control your weight!

3.
Proper Purse Organization Can Ease Strain, Reduce Risk

Many ladies continue to carry big purses with almost anything in them. About 75% is unnecessary to have every day, all day long. Even worse, the purse may end up weighing a lot and causing strain to the shoulders and back. Then, too, we don't want to be trying to manage a heavy purse that may attract a thief. It is much better to just carry what you must have in your purse.

Seniors should not carry check books, excessive charge cards, Medicare ID or Social Security cards. They should carry a driver's license, emergency contact information and medical alerts. Wallets are fine if they are compact. You do not want to keep anything in your purse that you cannot afford to lose. Expensive jewelry, treasured photos, or an excessive amount of cash are a no no! During the holidays, purse snatchers are watching for victims, particularly in store parking lots.

The best way to organize a purse is to dump everything out. Then group together similar items - make up, schedulers, snack items, jewelry, wallet, cleaning supplies, pens, keys, phone, note paper, pills, nail file, tissue, glasses, hand cream, gloves, etc. Only return to the purse the items you use at least multiple times a week – wallet, keys, phone, scheduler, pen, glasses, etc. Designate a spot in the purse for each item, particularly keys. Always return the items to the same spot. Keys should have one designated pocket.

For other items you need, but not in a purse, carry a second decorative bag. You can place shoes, scarves, notebooks, food or water in the second bag. You might even place your purse in it. Alternatively, keep many of the extra items in the car. It will be there when you need it.

If you really want to be extreme, lock your purse in your trunk and only carry your keys on a waistband key ring and one piece of ID. Unless you are shopping, there is no need to keep your purse with you. When visiting, exercising, attending church or events, go purse-less! Just remember – for safety's sake, only place your purse in your trunk, if you are driving away, never when you are walking away.

Enjoy feeling less vulnerable as you go about your daily business.

4.
Folders Help Keep Important Papers in Order

By the time we retire, we will have accumulated tons of paper – bank statements, bills, work/school documents, tax records, magazine articles, legal documents, etc. It is now time to scale down and organize the overwhelming collection of paper.

The secret of clearing paper whether in a file cabinet or folder is to start from the back. Pick a file cabinet drawer, go to the back of the drawer and start there. When you pull out the file folder to clear out, go to the back of the file folder. Generally, you will be looking at the oldest document, which in most cases will be obsolete. Remove it. Now continue reviewing from the back to the front removing the obsolete documents. Why do it this way? When you start from the back removing old documents, you set the momentum going. You will be in the mindset to trash, not save. If you start from the front you will be saving the documents; therefore, your mindset will be to save.

Nowadays, any pieces of paper with identifying information must be shredded or cut into very small pieces. You never want to leave yourself vulnerable to identity theft. Once the trash or recycling goes out front, who knows what might happen to it.

When setting up file folders, use broad categories instead of narrow groupings. Instead of setting up bills by name, just set up a broad category of bills. This will save space and reduce filing time.

To compress space in your filing system, open all documents to 8x11 size; don't leave them folded; save article pages, not the whole magazine; remove multiple copies, you only need one; and cut out foreign language sections of appliance/electronic/power machine instructions; better yet, trash all instructions after the item has been assembled.

If you want to get rid of more paper, start scanning your files to your computer. This can be a gigantic project, so do it by groupings, like reference material, articles, letters, etc.

With less paper to sort through it will be easy to find what you need quickly. Be sure to save your pages on a remote hard drive.

5.
Timers Can Help Keep You on Track

It seems when many older adults pass that sixty-five-year mark, it is so easy to get distracted. A spot on the floor catches your eye and you jump from unloading the dishwasher to cleaning the spot. For some, it is really hard to stay focused. Some of the distractions could cause dangerous consequences in the home, like leaving a stove burner on, neglecting to turn off the outside water or forgetting to pick up a grandchild from school.

To keep you on track, start using a timer. It can be a smartphone timer, kitchen timer, personal timer, or clock timer. Even if you know you will remember, set a timer when you turn on a burner. Set a timer for when the washer is going to end. Set a timer for moving or turning off the sprinkler. Set a timer if you need to depart in twenty minutes. Set a timer for how long you should shop at the grocery store or any store.

If you want to go to extremes, designate a block of time for each task and set your timer accordingly. For example: unloading the dishwasher is five minutes. Dusting the living room in thirty minutes. Grocery shopping or any retail shopping might be given two hours. Then you'll have time to read that book you always wanted to read.

By using a timer, it is easier to stay focused, simply because you know you have a deadline for your task. When the timer goes off, if you have not finished, you need to decide if you want to dedicate more time or just end the task unfinished. You may decide to continue the task at a later time; thus, resetting your timer.

You will have a great sense of accomplishment as you complete all your routine tasks and now can focus on the fun stuff.

6.
Sometimes, You Need a "Not to Do" List

Many seniors start every day with a "to do" list. Upon examining your list, you may find you are doing tasks too often and doing some tasks unnecessarily. Consider dusting and cleaning. Do you really need to do it every day or even every week? Can it be done just before company comes over or every other week? Also, do you need to cook food from scratch? Can you just buy lots of entrees from the supermarket that are already pre-cooked? Further, we do not have to prepare every meal (breakfast, lunch, dinner), every day. It is okay and even healthy to skip an occasional meal or just have a snack instead.

So, along with your "to do" list, also list what you will not do today. This is free time to either do nothing, which is still legal, or just relax. Items on the "not to do" list could include: not grocery shopping today, not doing paperwork today, not picking up the mail today, not returning calls today, or not watching TV today. Allowing yourself to not do something is freeing.

As an older adult, there are so many tasks we do not need to do, or at least, do by ourselves. When it comes to cooking, we can buy ready to cook or just go out to eat.

Let's consider lawn maintenance, cleaning and errands. Hire someone to cut your lawn, get a housekeeper to come regularly and ask your spouse, kids or friends to help out with errands. Next time the conversation turns to the holidays, see if a younger relative may want to host the big celebration.

We all know all the things we should do on a daily basis. But it is okay to only do the absolute minimal amount. Having fewer commitments reduces stress level. You will have more time for relaxing, and others will learn not to expect you to oversee everything. Maybe someone else needs to be the responsible person for a change!

The goal in life is to manage your time, not have time manage you.

7.
Write it Down So You Won't Forget

As we get older, our memory may fail us. At any time, our activities may require that we remember names, phone numbers, word spelling, an errand list, appointments, schedules and important dates. Also, we may need to recall where we placed a particular important item, money, or memorabilia. Or you may want to recall when an event occurred.

To stay organized, an appointment calendar works great. Even a daily to-do list can keep a senior on track for future appointments and events.

It is important to write down what you need to recall. If you just met a new acquaintance, write down his/her name. Write down phone numbers, emails, and addresses you will need to use or store them in your smartphone. If you are planning a vacation and need to list airline information for someone, write it down. How about a note to yourself on a project that you want to remember? If you write it on a sticky note, note pad, or business card, you may need to remember where you placed your note!

As a dedicated organizer, you keep a daily journal of events that occurred during a day. Maybe the lawn guy came, or the appliance repair person called to reschedule, or maybe you got sick during the night, or your grandchild got an award at school. So many significant events happen during a day that never get noted. In a journal, which can be a large spiral notebook or a small ledger, you can write down significant matters you want to remember. Here you can list phone numbers for all your calls for the day. New people you met and want to remember their names. Also, in a journal you can write your impression of an activity or the results of an event. If so inclined, you can keep all your sticky notes in the journal. A small news or a magazine article can be taped in the journal for future reference.

So, don't stress wondering where you hid your cash when you took a trip, or guess when the repairman came by, or dig for receipts regarding an item you purchased; just reference your journal.

Resolve to keep good notes in a journal. Events attended or planned for, purchases, luncheon dates, or just your thoughts about yourself or other loved ones.

8.
Find What You Want in Your Refrigerator

How often do you lose food in the refrigerator? When you do find it, has it spoiled?

Many older adults eat out often and bring home to-go trays. Also, when cooking for one, there will usually be leftovers. A senior's refrigerator may look like an accumulation of little packages, many with a surprise in it.

It is easy to place items in the refrigerator on any shelf, depending on space. So, when it is time to find the leftover piece of cake, we have no idea where that package was stored. To make things worse, it may be wrapped in aluminum foil, so you can't even see from the outside what is in the package. So, you end up opening multiple packages until you find the cake.

It is easy to know to store cheese and lunch meat in the dairy drawer and to place fruits and vegetables in the crisper, but everything else can be a free for all.

If left unorganized, you just cannot remember where items are in the refrigerator. To make it easier on yourself, start assigning types of food items to certain shelves and placing the items in long white mesh refrigerator baskets. There can be a basket for bread, dairy products, individual puddings and desserts, dinner leftovers, and fruits. The beauty of the basket plan is that nothing gets jammed in the back, because you pull the basket out if you need an item. Even better, when you are making a sandwich, you can pull out the breadbasket reviewing all your bread selections.

If you want to go more extreme, start storing vegetables in the crispers by shape. So, one crisper stores all round vegetables, like broccoli, onions and lettuce; the other one stores all oblong items like carrots, celery and green onions. You can get more in each crisper and don't have to guess or search as much.

By being organized, you will now be able to locate anything in your refrigerator at a glance. Further, with the basket organizers, you will not lose those special pieces of cake you brought home from the restaurant.

9.
Grocery Shopping: Pack Them Your Way

By the time you have reached retirement age, you may have made approximately 2000 weekly trips to the grocery shopping. (Fifty weeks a year x 40 years.) It is just a chore that has to be done. Since you do it so often, try to organize this task as efficiently as possible.

You can get more in your grocery cart if you organize it while you shop. Also, softer foods are protected from crushing, breaking and bruising. Designate a section for delicate items, cold items, small items, large boxes, and heavy items. Also keep fruits and vegetables together.

You may want to consider using a small hand basket or two in your grocery cart to keep cold items or produce together.

As an avid organizer you may want to pack your groceries as you shop in the recyclable bags. Fold the recyclable bags over so they will stay standing up. This also prevents overloading the bags. Now you may pack all your cold items in one bag, fruits in another bag, cleaning products in another bag, and so on.

When you are ready to check out, just lift each bag from your cart to the conveyer belt. The checker may be surprised, but just inform the person you want your groceries packed back into the same bag. The checker can pull out the items and return them to the same bag or they can have the packer repack the bag with the same items.

With the self-check, this system works just as well. You can have extra recyclable bags and just pull from the prepacked bag in the cart. You scan the items and place them in an empty recyclable bag.

Now, the perks just continue to grow. Not only do you have your bags packed precisely and neatly, but when you get home, you unpack them based on content. So, all your frozen items are ready for the freezer, breads are ready to go into the pantry or bread box, and all your cleaning products are together.

Now we can spend as little time as possible doing boring routine grocery shopping.

10.
Take the Mess Out of Trash

E veryone has trash. It can be paper intense, bulky, sticky, greasy, smelly and/or liquidly. So why not organize it? This way it will not be so unpleasant to deal with it. It used to be, way back when; we had simple trash and not that much. Trash would be food byproducts, metal, glass and maybe some plastic. Today, most of our trash is synthetic, made up of disposables – plastics, wrappings, paper products, styro-foam, etc. There is so much more of it today. Further, there is no organization to our trash. Food scraps are mixed with paper, mixed with grease, mixed with liquids.

We, as seniors, need to minimize the amount of our trash. So, it is best to organize the trash! Trash takes way too much space due to lack of compression. So, smashing the trash down in the container is a first step. Step two is to break down all bulk. Crush plastic containers, tear up boxes, and flatten paper before placing it in the trash receptacle or recycling container. Make the item as small as possible. Step three is to maximize the garbage disposal for unused food items.

Now if you want to be an extreme organizer, you go even further. Set up multipurpose trash containers – recyclable trash bin, rectangular can for nonrecyclable paper/plastic trash, and a container for round trash like bottles, jars and other circular items; for smelly perishables (chicken bones, onion skins, banana peel, pits) keep a container in the freezer. We all know how little critters are attracted to the smell of spoiled items. If you must place something messy in the trash can, grab one of those many small plastic bags we seem to accumulate and put the messy item in the small bag, seal it, and then trash it.

Make sure similar trash is kept together. Reducing trash to its smallest dimension eliminates multiple trips outside to the trash barrel. So, to keep your living quarters as sterile and fresh as possible, start giving your trash some thought before just tossing it.

II.
Is it Time to Reduce Paper in Your House?

Many older adults just can't part with their paper items. Now is the time to get rid of the excess. We continuously bring paper into the house. It could be mail, fliers, handouts, magazines, newspapers, and things we have saved over the years. We save books, articles, recipes, photos, greeting cards, old receipts, old records and paper memorabilia. In addition, we bring paper into the house via packaging, food trays and cups and disposable cleaning products.

It may be time to reduce the paper that fills up the house. Look at all the paper you already have in the house. Start with reading material – books, magazines, newspapers. Books are great to own and reference, but seniors should just keep a few and the rest can be donated to the library or hospitals. Magazines are fun to read, but after you are done, donate them to the local hospital or community center or your doctor. Newspapers should be placed in recycle bins. Even better, just go with digital versions of the daily news on your computer.

When you pick up the mail, presort it; place the bulk junk mail in the recycling before you enter your house. Notify companies sending you donation requests, catalogs or advertising to remove your name. Another alternative is to mark the mail "return to sender" and place it in the outgoing mail. Again, when you just come back from a vender fair or class, sort out the keepers from recycling as soon as you walk in the door.

If you are still saving all your articles, photos and greeting cards it may be time to reduce the paper memorabilia by scanning them. Old greeting cards can be donated to schoolteachers for children's craft projects. With paper memorabilia, like artwork, certificates, and diplomas, buy a frame and display some of them.

You do not have to save old receipts and records, generally, for more than seven years. Examine how often you have gone back beyond seven years. If you can't think of a reason to save old records, shred them.

Finally, cut down on paper household items. These mostly go to landfills. Check out your pretty linen towels, real plates and glasses. They are probably sitting in a cabinet or drawer collecting dust. It is just as easy to place a real dish in the dishwasher than to place a paper plate in the trash.

Reducing paper in the home will provide more space. More space means more tranquility.

12.
Store Belongings Behind Doors

D oors, cabinets and walls are available spaces that can be used for storage and/ or decorating.

Most living quarters have multiple doors. Generally, the doors have doorknobs. When organizing, the doorknobs can be used to hang hats, scarfs, hand towels, jackets or bags. The items are stored but out of the way and easily accessible.

If you want to consider vertical space organizing, every door back in your house can be used for storage. It is easy to purchase over-the-door hooks to store items behind the door.

For the bedroom closet or main entrance doors, one can purchase a specialized over-the-door hanger for an iron and ironing board, pockets for shoes and purse holders, scarf, tie, and belt rack, clothes hooks, craft storage, dressing mirror, even holiday wreaths can be stored nicely behind doors.

In the bathroom, over-the-door hooks can be used for towels or extra hanging bins for storage. A makeup mirror can also be hung behind the door. Even a magazine rack is a possibility.

Kitchen pantry doors can handle an over-the-door large spice/storage rack. Aprons, dish towels and plastic bags can be stored as well.

The inside of cabinet doors can be used to store notes, important lists or be used like a bulletin board. Further, keys hooks and mail racks can be installed. Some over-the-door spice racks will fit as well as paper towel holders, and organizers for plastic food keepers and lids.

Most homes have unused wall storage space. Walls in closets, kitchens, bedrooms and hallways can be converted into decorative storage spaces and display centers, and even memorabilia hubs. The combinations are as endless as your imagination.

So, don't spend lots of money for standalone storage units, be creative and use your vertical space.

13.
Shop at Home First

How often do you buy an item at the store, or order online, then later find you had a similar item stored in a cabinet or in the attic? We baby boomers do have a tendency to forget some of the things we own! At other times, coming up with a substitute can work just as well as a new item.

Stop before you shop! Shop at home first. Whether it is groceries, clothing, gifts or replacing broken appliances, you might find a duplicate or substitute in your own home.

Also, you don't always have to give something new from the store for celebrations or holidays. A treasured family item or the perfect gift for a friend might be right in your home.

Before grocery shopping survey your pantry, cabinets and refrigerator, you may find you already have the article, but have just forgotten about it. Cross off foods on your grocery list that you find. You may also find a large supply of a similar thing that would substitute just fine.

If the toaster breaks, use the toaster oven. If the coffee pot breaks, pull out the old one you stored that was working just fine. If the dishwasher messes up, call the repair man. No need to buy everything new.

As you are about to go clothes shopping, look in your closet at the items you do not wear often. Analyze why you don't wear those clothes. Are they too tight, too long, too big? Take them to your local dry cleaners to see if they can alter the apparel. It may work as a substitute.

A gift is a treasure you want to share with a loved one. Often, boomers have jewelry, keepsakes or other treasures ready to pass on to family or friends. You can gift these treasures for a special occasion or for no reason at all.

When it comes to repairs or replacements, as an older adult, it may not always be convenient to shop at a store or order online. So, check your supplies already at home, and I bet you will find something that will do the job.

14.
Additional Services Can Help Clear Clutter

As we get older, we should utilize services to allow us to stay in our home or living quarters. Services might include the lawn person, then a gardener, and then moving on to a housekeeper, etc. The service person we use most likely has all the equipment/tools needed to get the job done. So why are we keeping a duplicate set?

Now that you have a worker to cut your lawn and edge it, unclutter the garage and get rid of your lawn mower and edger. If a gardener does your flower beds, it is time to donate all your gardening tools, fertilizer and weed killer.

Have you gotten to the point where you hire a handyman to do your improvements and repairs? So, why keep all that lumber, scrap metal and tools? Save a few items for light maintenance and get rid of the bulk. This will clear up your garage or shed.

If you pay to belong to a gym, and go regularly, why hold on to those exercise weights, the stationary bike, or various exercise gadgets? Either sell or give away your unused equipment. The same applies to sports in which you no longer participate. Baseball mitts, fishing rods, camping tents, water floats are all cluttering up your living space. Give them away.

See if your children, grandchildren or neighbors may be happy to get them for free.

What if you eat out and seldom cook, do you really need to keep multiple sets of china or silverware? Many children do not want these items, consider selling them in a consignment shop. Lots of your pots, cooking dishes and appliances can be cleared out and donated. If you have a regular housekeeper cleaning your home, do you still need all your cleaning utensils– vacuum, shampooer, dusters? Even cleaning products can be put aside.

Why let items you no longer use continue to collect dust? Free up space so you can breathe and enjoy the pleasure of someone else doing the tough jobs.

15.
Organization Helps Manage Prescriptions

As a senior adult, whenever you go to the doctor the solution to the issue is too often another prescription. So, before you know it, you have multiple reoccurring pills to take. In addition, many of us may already use supplements like vitamins and minerals. Further, we all have our favorite over the counter regimen.

If you want to be organized, it is best to keep all medications together in one place, preferably a kitchen shelf. Separate over the counter medications from prescriptions on single or multilevel spinning spice racks. This way you always know the status of your supply. If you store in the kitchen, bedroom and bathroom, you really cannot assess your supply well. If you have grandchildren who might get into the drugs, you should find a safe, and even locked, cabinet.

If you can, use a computer-generated mail order system, you will find this is the most efficient. For reoccurring prescriptions, a 90-day supply is most economical. Many of the computerized mail order systems prompt you when you are due to run out.

When it is time to fill up your weekly AM/PM pill case, gather all your pharmacy pill bottles. Rather than fill one pill case for a week, fill 4-5 for a month or more. This process works best if two people fill the pill cases. One person counts out the pills needed, and the other places them in the pill cases. When the pill bottle is nearly empty, it is now time to renew the online 90-day order. With this system, you never run out, because you are ordering at least 30 days before you need the medication.

As an extreme organizer, also maintain a computerized spreadsheet of all your medications with the generic name, brand name, dosage amount and time taken (morning, afternoon, evening). On your list you can alpha/numerically code medication, and then do the same for the bottle. Aspirin could be #1 on the spreadsheet, so you would code the cap of aspirin with #1. Color coding also can work.

Not taking the right medication amount at the right time can be a life-threatening issue. Keep yourself safe by keeping your prescriptions well organized.

16.
Organize for a Smooth Trip

It used to be, for many of us boomers, when we traveled, everything seemed to go well with little effort. Now it seems like between getting lost, forgetting or misplacing things, and overall confusion, trips often seem more stressful. It is important to plan and organize before traveling. When retirees travel, more incidentals are needed: like medications, band aides, creams/lotions and medical equipment, such as a blood pressure cuff.

Before leaving, make a checklist of everything you need to bring. Start grouping items for travel at least two days prior to leaving. Make sure you make a copy of all of the important documents to carry with you and to leave for an emergency contact.

When packing your suitcase, use mesh or plastic zipper bags for various groups of clothing – pants, shirts, jackets and underwear. Keep makeup, toiletries and medicines in clear plastic zipper bags, also. Get travel size toiletries to conserve space. Minimize items you bring, because too many things soon get heavy and disorganized. Place identification labels on your cell phone, tablet, camera and carryon baggage.

When in your room at a hotel, organize items that you take out of your suitcase – designate the desk for money, wallet, purse; end table for food items; and the dresser top for sunglasses, cameras and cell phones. Try not to scatter clothing and packages all over the room.

As retirees travel, it can be irritating to discover that the city maps have very small print, hotel safes are low to the floor and require a lot of maneuvering to open, and showers can be very small and tight.

Be super prepared to avoid accidents, theft, and delays. The more you plan and organize for travel, the more enjoyable and relaxing you will find your vacation.

17.
Get Organized Before You Drive

As seniors, every time we get into our automobile, we need to be prepared for grocery shopping, bad weather, car problems and traffic delays. Organizing before your trips will alleviate stress and panic.

Regularly check to see that you have your registration and insurance card. Never leave your home without your cell phone. It is as essential as your driver's license. In addition, know whom you will call if you need a tow due to an engine problem or an accident. Keep the phone number of someone who will help you (relative or friend) and your local auto repair shop contact.

As an organized senior, you should not use your car for storage or for eating, drinking, or smoking. All of these acts make the car seem unkept. Not to mention the chance for a spill to stain clothing.

Cars should be kept in a garage when not in use, so they are protected against bad weather and theft.

Before doing your weekly shopping or visit to friends, check to see that you have everything you need. Cloth bags can be kept in the trunk. In hot weather, it is a good idea to permanently have an ice chest in the trunk for cold/frozen food items for your trip home. If you have space in your trunk, keep large sturdy bins or crates to place your grocery bags so they will stand up.

In case there's a change in weather, keep sunglasses, umbrella, flashlight, blanket or sweater available to grab as needed. In case of an unforeseen auto problem or a crash, keep paper and pen stored in your glove compartment, and, in the trunk or back of a SUV, keep starter cables, air pump, bottled water and some bungee cords. Finally keep a full-size spare tire in the trunk if possible, not the donut tires. As a senior, this will reduce stress when you find yourself in a jam.

The more prepared and organized you are each time you leave the house, the easier it will be to get back home safely.

18.
Organize Your Home's Garage

C ontrary to popular practice, garages are for cars. Before baby boomers know it, the cars are parked in the driveway and the garage is used for storage. It is best to calculate how much space is needed for the cars, then the remaining area can be used to store outdoor items. The items stored in the garage should be garden and work tools, auto supplies, and outdoor sports equipment. No indoor items should be stored in the garage, and, for sure, no broken household items.

Install over the head shelves for storing bulky objects. Any household objects that are seldom used should be moved to the attic. If needed, buy a shed or rent an outdoor storage locker. Get rid of objects that have not been used in the last three years. Use the area on the back wall near the home entrance for keeping a tool chest, installing a work bench and storing the lawn mower, leaf blower, lawn food spreader, etc. Use the side walls for additional shelves and for hanging lawn tools.

When the cars are out of the garage during the day, you can use the garage as an extra work area. As an extremely organized boomer, the garage can be lined with outdoor carpet and be used as a covered patio.

Also, feel free to decorate the garage so that it feels more like part of the house. Decorate with a wreath on the door into the house, posters or cheap paintings on the walls and even a ceiling fan. The more purposeful the garage looks, the less chance it will end up as a storage locker.

19.
Unclutter Your Living Space

Uncluttering is a necessity for retirees. If you don't do it, your loved ones will be left with this task. It is up to you to get rid of all the meaningless junk around the home. Meaningless junk is for the retiree to decide. It could be old documents, magazines, household and outdoor items, etc. It could also be valuables like china, crystal or jewelry no one wants.

If you have items you have not used or looked at in ten years, an appliance that does not work, or you have duplicates, or even triplicates, of the same thing, or you forgot you owned this object in the first place, it is time to dispose of the item. Ask yourself the question: Why am I saving this? If the answer is: I might need it someday with no reasonable expectation of when that will be, then it is time to get rid of the item.

Keep objects you are still using, even if only occasionally. Keep anything you know someone will want after you are gone.

Uncluttering is a process, not a one-time shot. Before you know it, stuff starts sneaking back into the house, and you don't even notice it. Maybe, you purchase it as a replacement, or it was a good deal you felt you couldn't pass up, or a gift.

Here are some general steps to unclutter any area:

Step 1 – Pitch any trash.

Step 2 – Return all things to a designated place.

Step 3 – Decide on focus. This can be largest item, one section of your home.

Step 4 - Separate keepers and removables.

Step 5 – Get rid of removables from the home as soon as possible.

Repeat Steps 3 - 5.

Ask someone younger or stronger to work with you. It is more fun when people work together, and if you have to lift or move something, it is nice to have help. As your undesirable items are removed from the house, you will take pride in your new-found space.

20.
Move Clutter Out of Your House

There are various traditional methods of disposing of items no longer wanted. You can start with just utilizing the weekly trash pick-up. In certain areas, furniture and the like gets picked up per your garbage pick-up schedule, or you can break down a large item and place it in the trash barrel.

Any documents with personal identity information need to be shredded. This includes mail, tax returns, bills, etc. Everyone should own a shredder.

Many neighborhoods have community garage sales, or you can have your own. Be aware that buyers are looking for bargains, so you will generally receive a minimal price. Be sure to have a cash box for making change.

Goodwill, Salvation Army or other charities take household items, furniture, and clothing in good shape. Place an ad to advertise the sale of more valuable things on websites like Craigslist, newspapers or bulletin boards. There are companies that will haul your excess belongings away, and you will never be bothered again; but be prepared to pay a hefty price.

Finally, if you have an item that has a true market value, consider a consignment store or pawn shop.

Some non-traditional methods of disposing of items include the following:

Return - If you bought something that did not work out or it was undesirable, return it!

Many stores will take back items with or without a receipt. If you don't have a receipt, check to see if the store will give you credit. You have nothing to lose by asking.

Gift - It is not awful to give a treasure as a gift. You can use a special occasion or no reason at all. Gift those treasures to relatives or friends. If someone admires something you have wanted to get out of the house, give it to them.

Trade - You may be able to find someone willing to trade a service you need for something you need to get rid of as payment. Someone may be willing to do garden work in trade for garden tools you own.

Mail - If you have someone who will take a small item, don't hold on to it until they come to get it, instead place it in a box and mail it.

Take a picture - Some items are just too bulky, dirty or old to keep. Take a picture for a memory and then trash the item or have it carried off.

This certainly is not an overnight task. Uncluttering can take years. The idea is to find good homes for your belongings that you once loved and enjoyed. For the items you have no sentiment for, just send them on their way by whatever means.

21.
Keep It Differently This Time

When an individual is in the process of uncluttering, there will be many items that will be kept. You will need to decide how you will keep each item. You certainly do not want to keep cherished items stored in a box, never to be used or viewed.

Display - If you have decorative items, frame them or display them on the wall. It is easy to display certificates, gifts, religious icons and paintings, etc. This way you enjoy viewing the item and it is not hidden away, seldom to be seen. You can also make decorative centerpieces for your home or as gifts.

Redesign - It is easy to redesign clothes or linens to extend their usefulness. All types of clothes and linens can be reused in a different form. For clothes, change the collar, sleeves, pant length, and you have an updated outfit. Linens can be converted to other fabric items like potholders, table runners, or linen decorations. If you are going to keep it, get some use out of it. If you do not sew, take the item to a cleaner that does alterations and you will get some more use out of loved clothing and linens.

Compress - Certain items can be compressed in a tighter, smaller form. Use bags that remove the air and reduce the bulk of items, particularly for blankets and bulky clothes. Fold items to make them as small as possible. This works great for blankets, bedspreads, sleeping bags, pillows, etc.

Repair - If there is something you love that is broken – appliance, china plate, knickknack, or a wall hanging, focus on getting it repaired. Sometimes it is more prudent to repair than to replace, particularly if you love the item. Get favorite furniture reupholstered, re-caned or refinished. If it cannot be repaired, trash it.

Hide - If you insist on keeping an item, but can't think of anything else to do, hide it. Install shelves high in the closet. Place items you can't part with, but never use, on these shelves. Also, you can hide items in the back of kitchen cabinets that are hard to access. Just mark the box of what you store, so you do not have to open it to see what is inside. There may come a day when you will find a home for these hidden items.

Keep in mind, you, as an older adult, are the only one who knows your belongings. If you become disabled, sick or die, a loved one will need to deal with all the stuff you never got to review. How wonderful to leave your loved ones the gift of organization!

22.
Control Your Spending by Organizing

Every senior adult should have a good grip on his or her spending habits. Whether you have a little bit or a lot of money, seniors should be knowledgeable of where their money goes.

At least once a year, assess your financial wellness. Do you feel comfortable with your income? Do you need to look for more income? The bigger question is do you even know how much annual income you have? Is an accountant or someone else handling all your finances? You should ask questions, so you know where you stand.

As an exercise, record all your spending, savings and losses for a three month period. When you save on a deal, track it, but also track your losses. Losses are usually the result of a bad spending decision.

Seniors should prepare a simple annual budget. During the month of December, plan a budget for the next year. This gives you a general idea of what you can afford the coming year. It does not take long for expenses to add up. This is a good time to consider changes to your spending habits.

Every family should review the following annually:

Insurance – Home, Auto, Life, Accident, Medical, Supplements

Charge Accounts – Interest Rate, Balance, Usage, Names on Accounts

Discretionary Expenses – Food, Clothes, Vacation, Gas, Gifts, TV Cable

There are new money rules when you become a senior. Many of us have worked for close to fifty years, so make sure you collect your entitlements. You paid for them through your taxes. Never bypass a refund/adjustment/ return. If you don't follow up, you will be leaving a lot of money on the table. As a senior, use the "fixed income" card, and ask for a better deal or discount at many locations. Finally, be aware of the tax consequences of your spending. The government never stops reaching out for its share of your money.

Good organizing and planning of spending will allow you to get the most out of the money you have available to you.

23.
Get Ready to Sort by Pattern

Patterns can be used to simplify decorating and utilizing your home space. So, when organizing, a senior can pick a variety of patterns to organize their living space. Organizing can be done by shape, size, color, length, texture, purpose, use, cost, relationship, alphabetical, numerical, or linear grouping.

In the closet, seniors may want to organize clothing by type, length, color, or texture. Blouses with long sleeves or all black color pants can be maintained together. The same type of shoes could be kept together. Organize your dresser drawers by relationship.

Underclothes can be in one drawer, makeup can be together, and toiletries together.

For the man, a similar pattern can be employed for manly items.

In the kitchen, you can organize the pantry shelves by shape; storing rectangular boxes on the left and round cans on the right or on different shelves entirely. In your refrigerator, similar purposed items can be stored together; like vegetables, dairy products, and leftovers. Kitchen drawers can be organized by use. All cooking tools can be kept together by use. All dishware may be stored by shape. Store your spices alphabetically. Store vitamins and medicines by a numbering system with a sheet explaining the medicine assigned to the number.

Linen closets can be organized by texture. Kitchen towels can be kept separate from bath towels. Also, linens can be organized by size.

In a woman's jewelry case, organize by cost and relationship. All your expensive jewels are kept together, while matching sets of costume jewelry are stored by relationship and style.

In the garage, store all your tools by purpose: painting, woodworking, or gardening. Automobile products like windshield washer, gas can, sponges, etc. should be kept close together.

Group similar trash together. Recyclables can be grouped together. When possible, sort trash by shape and type. Compress it, so you have less to take out.

Identifying an organizing pattern and applying it to your home will allow you to work more efficiently and effectively in your living space. Also, you will be able to find items you use together without looking all through the house.

24.
Here's How You Can Maintain an Uncluttered Home and Life

As a retiree, you have now uncluttered your living space, but how do you maintain this newly acquired freedom? You will need to work just as hard to keep your space uncluttered as you did un-cluttering it.

Begin by changing your shopping patterns. Only shop when you need something. Check your pantry, cabinet and closet first. If you find something that will work instead of shopping for a similar thing, use it first. When you do shop, stop buying in bulk. The more you buy, the more clutter you have to care for in your home. Buy what you need and in a handy size. In most large cities, there are grocery or retail stores within one to two miles. Make a list of what you need and just shop when you are about to run out. No stocking pantries to overflowing!

It is now time to stop accepting freebees and leave the bargains and markdowns for someone else. When attending events like vendor fairs, classes, or day excursions, leave the handouts and promotional gifts behind. Unless you know you will consume a product, don't take it. With handouts, just take what you are really interested in. You can always research information on the computer. When shopping at retail stores, minimize taking the bargains. If you buy too much, you may regret it.

If you are getting too much through the mail, keep notifying charities, catalog companies, and coupon venders that you want the mailings to stop going to your address. Also, start paying bills online and check your accounts via the computer. If you order magazines, make sure you peruse and dispose of the current month before the next month's copy arrives.

When some household item breaks, the first thought should be repair, not replace. Give every item, at the minimum, one repair. Some repairs you can do yourself. Use glue, needles and thread, or duct tape to keep things going just a little longer. If you must replace it, dispose of the broken item first, so it does not add to cluttering the house.

To continue to reduce untidiness, stop buying, and start renting or borrowing. For

DVDs you can rent from Red Box or just check out the movie from the library. If you need a ladder once in a while, borrow it from a neighbor. Hire a handy man who will have all the tools needed for a household job. When you hire a service, you are renting their time and equipment. You might even want to lease, instead of owning a car. Better yet, use Uber or Lyft services. No need to keep multiple cars.

Maintaining an uncluttered house is like living on a healthy food plan. You have to work on it every day. Once in a while you may slip up, but you need to get back to the plan the next day. Venders and retailers want you to keep buying. It increases profits for them, but why buy things you don't absolutely have to have?

25.
Staying Organized: Choices for Simple Living

The expression, "You can't take it with you!" becomes more real as you get older. Living simply prepares you to scale down to the items you love and use often. The less stuff, the more freedom you have.

Seniors may choose to live a simple lifestyle for various reasons. Some live it because their income demands it; possibly some are caring for loved ones; others are tired of all the stuff and its maintenance. Still others, may do it for religious reasons or a strong conservationist belief. Whatever the reason, it involves reducing consumption, possessing less, conserving energy and respecting time.

So how do you get to simple living?

Unclutter – Get rid of excess items, duplicates, broken items. Only keep what you have used in the last three years. You could start getting rid of camping items, lawn mowers, duplicate pots, and extra china sets. Go through your whole house and garage.

Organize – Keep the items you use orderly so you can find them easily. Keep similar items together. Keep articles you use the most often nearby. Everything should be assigned a place, and it should always be returned to the designated place. Never go to bed without replacing items to their proper place.

Stop before you shop – Whether it is grocery shopping, clothes shopping, or Christmas shopping, stop and assess what you already have. Check the pantry, closets, shelves, and, in some cases, the attic. You may already have something that will work instead of buying new. You don't always have to get something new. Consider alternatives to buying products. Only buy what you need, not excess.

Reduce use of paper products and disposables – Be environmentally friendly. Use recyclable bags, glass and crockery dishes and cups, and cloth napkins. As an environmentally friendly person, reduce use of plastics, papers products, and styro-foam. This includes items for meals, shopping, and entertainment.

Start Saying "No" – Stop feeling obligated to go along with doing things you despise. Only participate in events you like and have fun doing. Simplify your daily life by picking and choosing your commitments. You no longer need to feel obligated to attend and sponsor all the events you have in the past.

Participate in what gives you the most pleasure and let the other events go. Living simply gives you more space, fewer obligations, and satisfaction that you are helping the environment. Your time can now be spent doing your favorite things. With all this clarity, you will find peace of mind and the spark of joy that living well brings.

26.
Your Routine: Organize Items for Daily Convenience

As a general rule, most older adults follow the same routine day in and day out. It is a good idea to examine the daily routine to see if it can be improved. Since many of us have a reduced level of energy, why not make the daily tasks as simple and convenient as possible.

In the kitchen, you want the pots, spices, etc. that you use daily to be close by and easy to access. Counter tops should be for appliances used daily, like coffee pots and toasters ovens. Counter tops should be clear of non-essential décor. If you use a tea kettle every day, leave it out, if not, store it in the kitchen cabinet.

When you look at your closet, do you find hundreds of pieces of clothes, but only wear about ten percent? If that is the case, move your occasional clothes to a storage closet. Your main clothes closet should be only for clothes you wear regularly. By selecting out clothing seldom worn, it will be easier to maintain and review your wardrobe.

As we get older, medications become more important to administer correctly. For convenience sake, it is best to keep all prescriptions and over the counter pills together in the same cabinet in the kitchen. A Lazy Susan type tray will allow you to spot the right pill container when searching. Pills should be at eye level, not too high or too low.

In the bathroom, daily toiletries should all be within reach. A container with a handle that contains all lotions, makeup, and creams can be gathered together. When needed, just pull out the toiletry container or just keep it visible on the counter.

For convenience's sake, refrigerators should only hold foods needing refrigeration and not used for general storage. This will allow more visibility. Compress packaging as much as possible, so you can quickly locate what you want for meals.

Finally, keep your cars in the garage. It is much more convenient when the weather is bad to be under a roof than walk out into the elements. When planning your trips, you can easily place things like luggage in the car without worrying that someone will be stealing your goods. Even better, when your vehicle is in the garage you don't have to constantly lock it.

The easier you make it for yourself on routine tasks, the more time you will have for the grandkids and other social activities. Don't get bogged down with the routine drudgery.

27.
Go Small, Easier to Handle

Living in Texas, everything is big. For seniors in retirement, big is often too cumbersome. The days of big houses, big furniture, big parties and big meals make little sense.

Start with shopping. Stop buying bulk! Bulk is not always the cheapest. The more you have, the more you end up wasting because of the items expiring. In time, bulk foods get dry and messy; then, you get tired of eating the same food. Buy small, handy size items. A one to three- month supply is good.

Look in your closet, and you will notice you wear the same clothes and jewelry. Much apparel is only used occasionally. Go small in your closet. You can now use a smaller space in your closet if you rid yourself of some clothing.

Go small in your living quarters. Look for smaller furniture, multipurpose appliances and tools, and decorate less. The less furniture and fewer decorations you have, the less you need to clean and dust. You may find yourself moving from a home to an apartment to maybe an assisted living facility, so be prepared.

Go small with meals. No need for extra-large anything. At this point in our life, we should be eating less and better.

Order a small portion or child's portion or split your meal with your spouse or friend. Reduce junk foods and sweets. You probably have had your fill during your lifetime.

Go small and practical with your vehicle. Maybe leasing a vehicle will be the best way to go. Minimize luxury, showy cars. Don't be a target for thieves. If your driving is restricted, pay for Uber/Lyft instead of making a car payment, car insurance, and dealing with parking headaches.

Smaller is easier to handle. Smaller means less maintenance. Smaller is less expensive. Give yourself the gift of less hassle.

28.
Conclusion

The expression, "You can't take it with you" is an actuality when you die. So, start now distributing your valued jewels, memorabilia, and art work and trashing your junk. It is easier for you to do it, rather than leaving the task for spouses, children and grandchildren. Keep a few items you really enjoy. Distribute the rest. You won't miss all the excess and can focus on the things that give you pleasure.

In my spare time, I visit residents at nursing homes, senior living facilities and senior apartments. It has become clear to me that senior adults will eventually need to scale down. Rather than waiting till you are no longer able to make decisions about your belongings, start right after retirement and scale down. Take classes, read books, and recruit your family and friends to help with discarding that which you don't need. As a reward, gift items that your helpers are interested in owning. You enjoyed the various items for years, so it is now time to pass treasures on. As cruel as it sounds: We came into this world with nothing and we will leave with nothing!

It can be really enjoyable gifting many of your prized things and just finding the right spot for what needs to go away. There is just the right person or group that will appreciate and care for the item.

Hold on to items that are meaningful to you. Enjoy disbursing the rest. Peace to all.

End

Made in the USA
Middletown, DE
28 September 2021